W9-AZG-588

Y
390
9 BON

WITHDRAWN

7/04 Pub, 22.95
BEAMAN MEMORIAL
PUBLIC LIBRARY
West Boylston, Massachusetts

Christmas and Santa Claus Folklore

North American Folklore

Children's Folklore
Christmas and Santa Claus Folklore
Contemporary Folklore
Ethnic Folklore
Family Folklore
Firefighters' Folklore
Folk Arts and Crafts
Folk Customs
Folk Dance
Folk Fashion
Folk Festivals
Folk Games
Folk Medicine
Folk Music
Folk Proverbs and Riddles
Folk Religion
Folk Songs
Folk Speech
Folk Tales and Legends
Food Folklore
Regional Folklore

North American Folklore

Christmas and Santa Claus Folklore

BY SHERRY BONNICE

Mason Crest Publishers

Mason Crest Publishers Inc.
370 Reed Road
Broomall, Pennsylvania 19008
(866) MCP-BOOK (toll free)
www.masoncrest.com

Copyright © 2003 by Mason Crest Publishers. All rights reserved. No part of this publication may be reproduced or transmitted in any form or by any means, electronic or mechanical, including photocopying, recording, taping, or any information storage and retrieval system, without permission from the publisher.

First printing
1 2 3 4 5 6 7 8 9 10
Library of Congress Cataloging-in-Publication Data on file at the Library of Congress.
ISBN 1-59084-330-4
        1-59084-328-2 (series)

Design by Lori Holland.
Composition by Bytheway Publishing Services, Binghamton, New York.
Cover design by Joe Gilmore.
Printed and bound in the Hashemite Kingdom of Jordan.

Picture credits:
Corbis: pp. 6, 12, 15, 18, 44, 56, 61, 63, 90
Corel: pp. 16, 30, 53, 54, 70, 72, 92
Image Ideas: pp. 34, 37, 40, 52, 64, 69, 71, 74, 76, 81, 83
PhotoDisc: pp. 38, 100
Cover: "Santa Reading Mail" by Norman Rockwell © 1935 SEPS: Licensed by Curtis Publishing, Indianapolis, IN. www.curtispublishing.com

Printed by permission of the Norman Rockwell Family
© the Norman Rockwell Family Entities

Contents

Folklore grows from long-ago
seeds. Just as an acorn sends
down roots even as it shoots up
leaves across the sky, folklore is
rooted deeply in the past and
yet still lives and grows today.
It spreads through our modern
world with branches as wide
and sturdy as any oak's;
it grounds us in yesterday even
as it helps us make sense of
both the present and the future.

Introduction

by Dr. Alan Jabbour

WHAT DO A TALE, a joke, a fiddle tune, a quilt, a jig, a game of jacks, a saint's day procession, a snake fence, and a Halloween costume have in common? Not much, at first glance, but all these forms of human creativity are part of a zone of our cultural life and experience that we sometimes call "folklore."

The word "folklore" means the cultural traditions that are learned and passed along by ordinary people as part of the fabric of their lives and culture. Folklore may be passed along in verbal form, like the urban legend that we hear about from friends who assure us that it really happened to a friend of their cousin. Or it may be tunes or dance steps we pick up on the block, or ways of shaping things to use or admire out of materials readily available to us, like that quilt our aunt made. Often we acquire folklore without even fully realizing where or how we learned it.

Though we might imagine that the word "folklore" refers to cultural traditions from far away or long ago, we actually use and enjoy folklore as part of our own daily lives. It is often ordinary, yet we often remember and prize it because it seems somehow very special. Folklore is culture we share with others in our communities, and we build our identities through the sharing. Our first shared identity is family identity, and family folklore such as shared meals or prayers or songs helps us develop a sense of belonging. But as we grow older we learn to belong to other groups as well. Our identities may be ethnic, religious, occupational, or regional—or all of these, since no one has only one cultural identity. But in every case, the identity is anchored and strengthened by a variety of cultural traditions in which we participate and share with our neighbors. We feel the threads of connection with people we know, but the threads extend far beyond our own immediate communities. In a real sense, they connect us in one way or another to the world.

Folklore possesses features by which we distinguish ourselves from each other. A certain dance step may be African American, or a certain story urban, or a certain hymn Protestant, or a certain food preparation Cajun. Folklore can distinguish us, but at the same time it is one of the best ways we introduce ourselves to each other. We learn about new ethnic groups on the North American landscape by sampling their cuisine, and we enthusiastically adopt musical ideas from other communities. Stories, songs, and visual designs move from group to group, enriching all people in the process. Folklore thus is both a sign of identity, experienced as a special marker of our special groups, and at the same time a cultural coin that is well spent by sharing with others beyond our group boundaries.

Folklore is usually learned informally. Somebody, somewhere, taught us that jump rope rhyme we know, but we may have trouble remembering just where we got it, and it probably wasn't in a book that was assigned as homework. Our world has a domain of formal knowledge, but folklore is a domain of knowledge and culture that is learned by sharing and imitation rather than formal instruction. We can study it formally—that's what we are doing now!—but its natural arena is in the informal, person-to-person fabric of our lives.

Not all culture is folklore. Classical music, art sculpture, or great novels are forms of high art that may contain folklore but are not themselves folklore. Popular music or art may be built on folklore themes and traditions, but it addresses a much wider and more diverse audience than folk music or folk art. But even in the world of popular and mass culture, folklore keeps popping up around the margins. E-mail is not folklore—but an e-mail smile is. And college football is not folklore—but the wave we do at the stadium is.

This series of volumes explores the many faces of folklore throughout the North American continent. By illuminating the many aspects of folklore in our lives, we hope to help readers of the series to appreciate more fully the richness of the cultural fabric they either possess already or can easily encounter as they interact with their North American neighbors.

The Christmas season pulls together many traditions; some have their roots in Christianity, while others come from more ancient practices.

ONE

The Christ Child
The Gift of Light

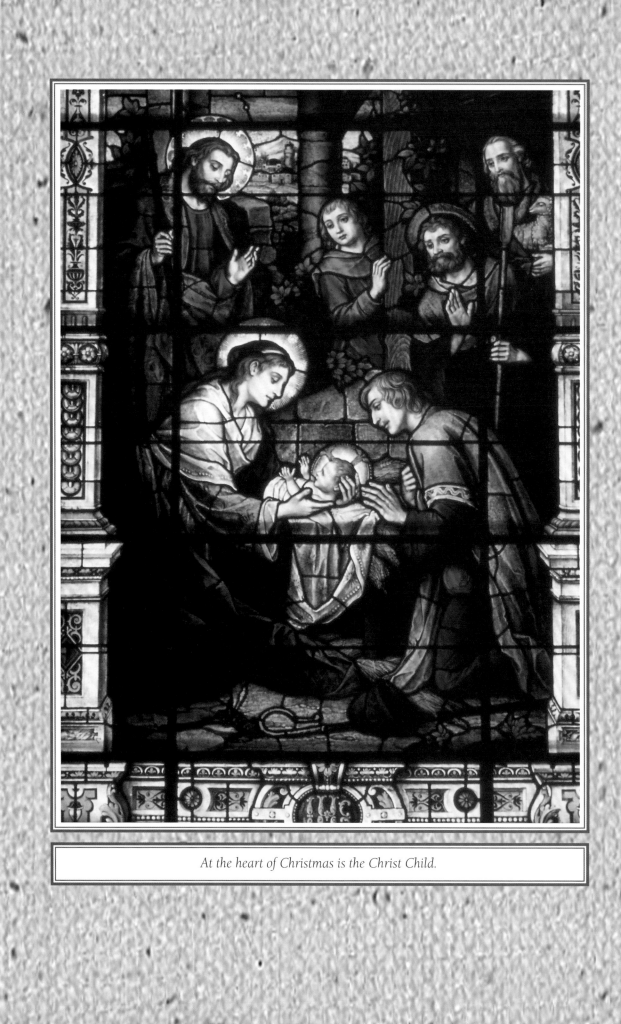

At the heart of Christmas is the Christ Child.

WHILE THEY WERE *there, the time came for the baby to be born, and she gave birth to her firstborn, a son. She wrapped him in cloths and placed him in a manger, because there was no room for them in the inn. And there were shepherds living out in the fields nearby, keeping watch over their flocks at night. An angel of the Lord appeared to them, and the glory of the Lord shone around them, and they were terrified. But the angel said to them, "Do not be afraid. I bring you good news of great joy that will be for all the people. Today in the town of David a Savior has been born to you; he is Christ the Lord. This will be a sign to you: You will find a baby wrapped in cloths and lying in a manger.* (Luke 2:6–12)

Christmas is the holiday of giving. This spirit of generosity and **benevolence** is rooted in the legend of a lowly stable. There, more than 2,000 years ago, the Christ Child was born, bringing to earth the gift of everlasting life.

Rooted in this biblical account, Christmas is an ancient holiday; it has been celebrated in many ways for many years. Our Christmas celebrations today are far different from those of 500 years ago, or even 100 years ago. Today Christmas is a commercial season that puts money in the pockets of businesses and department stores across North America—but the Christmas season continues to honor the divine gift of the Christ Child.

Christmas is the time of the year when most people remember those they love with special keepsakes. They share tokens of gratitude with persons who provide a year of services. Gifts and cards are sent to friends and family who are far away. Donations

 are contributed to those in need. People everywhere experience the joy of giving.

Although Christmas is recognized as the birthday of Jesus Christ, historically, Jesus probably was not born on December 25th. (In fact, he may have been born in the spring.) Early Christians, however, sought to unite the celebration of Christ's birth with other older celebrations.

These festivals are rooted in ancient beliefs. The winter *solstice*, the shortest day of the year, falls around December 21— and early cultures feared this time of short days and long, dark nights. They wondered if they might be punished by losing the sun forever. Their winter solstice rituals were intended to "call the sun back." Torches and candles shone brightly at these celebrations, and feasts and games added to the fun. Gifts were given, but back then it was the rich who gave to the poor and the slaves. This happy occasion brightened the lives of those who served their masters throughout the year.

In the early Christian era, another religious belief vied for popularity with Christianity. Many Romans worshipped Mithra, a Persian savior-god. His birth was celebrated on December 25th, and the festival was called the "Birthday of the Unconquered Son." There were many parallels between Mithra and Jesus, and in the fourth century AD, Christians adopted Mithra's birthday as Jesus'.

There were good reasons for doing this. Like the earlier solstice celebrations, Jesus' birth was also associated with light. A light had shone around the angels who appeared to the shepherds telling them the good news of his birth, and a brilliant star guided the **Magi** on their journey to worship the newborn king.

Today, Jesus the "Light of the World" is symbolized by the glowing candles of Christmas. Many churches hold candlelight services on Christmas Eve; people light candles in windows and on tabletops; and even the bright lights that decorated houses and trees are symbols of the divine light that came to earth.

Today people often claim that we have "lost the true meaning of Christmas." They look back fondly at their childhood Christmases, believing that Christmas was somehow more "real," more traditional, back when they were young. Actually, however, our modern world has its own traditions; some of these may be a bit different from those our parents and grandparents enjoyed, but they are nevertheless still tied to customs and beliefs that stretch all the way back to that long-ago birth.

Our world is not the first to have difficulty keeping the spirit of Christmas fresh in our minds. The light of generosity and divine love has always been easily obscured by human greed and selfishness. Somehow, though, the light continues to burn, century after century.

In the **Middle Ages**, people were not so very different from what they are today: they enjoyed the festivities of Christmas, but they easily forgot the meaning behind the celebration. According to an old folk legend, Francis of Assisi wanted desperately to make the Christmas story live in people's hearts forever. Although he was born the son of a rich Italian merchant, Francis had forsaken his life of leisure to care for those who were poor and needy. He was well known for his preaching, and people came long distances to hear him.

A crèche is a scene made to represent the Nativity, the birth of Jesus. The story of Saint Francis's first crèche led to the creation of miniature nativities as a popular part of the Christmas celebrations in homes and churches throughout North America and the world. Today, live nativities are also popular, especially on Christmas Eve.

Saint Francis of Assisi used a crèche like this to bring the Gospel stories alive.

One evening very close to Christmas, Francis came upon shepherds in the fields tending their flocks. The words from the Bible in the second chapter of Luke came to him: "And there were shepherds living out in the fields nearby, keeping watch over their flocks at night." Suddenly, he knew what he would do to help people remember the story of Jesus' birth.

With the help of his friend Giovanni, Francis prepared the church for the Christmas Eve service. As the worshippers entered, they fell to their knees. Before them was the manger scene, including a live ox and donkey. The figures of Jesus, Mary,

In Rome the most famous *presepi* (crèche in Italian) is 45 feet long, 21 feet wide, and 27 feet high with hundreds of wooden, hand-carved figurines that include an angel waking a shepherd who has fallen asleep. Herod is also seen pointing the way to Bethlehem for the Wise Men, and there are hills, valleys, and lighted villages. At the center, of course, the Holy Family celebrates the birth of Jesus.

Joseph, and the shepherds may have been played by townspeople or they may have been carved of wood; either way, seeing the story laid out before them in three dimensions made it come alive for the worshippers that night. As Francis related to the people the story of Christ's birth, those who listened felt that they too had visited the tiny Baby in Bethlehem.

The story of Jesus' birth has been told in many languages through songs, poems, plays, and paintings. Countless folk traditions, folktales, and folksongs have sprung out of this single story, and the legends that have risen around Jesus' birth abound. From talking farm animals who speak on Christmas Eve, to kings who travel from afar to give gifts, these tales of giving have grasped the human imagination for generations.

Saint Nicholas came to represent the generosity of the Gospels' message.

In Bethlehem, Pennsylvania, the descendants of Moravian and Bohemian immigrants celebrate with the Christmas *putz* (crèche). Along with large community scenes, individuals include a putz in their homes. The practice of "putz-visiting" begins on Christmas Eve and continues throughout holy week. Besides enjoying each other's nativity scenes, food and fellowship abound.

In the fifth century AD, in the region then known as Asia Minor, a man named Nicholas was so influenced by the Christmas story, that he, like Francis of Assisi, lived his entire life by its light. When he heard that a merchant in his community planned to sell his oldest daughter into slavery in order to pay his debts, Nicholas responded with generosity.

Late one night, he filled a bag with gold and then hurried through the dark streets to the merchant's house. He tossed the bag through a smoke hole in the chimney and then crept away without being seen. According to legend, the merchant's three daughters had washed their stockings the night before and hung them by the fire to dry. Nicholas's gold landed in their stockings—and when they showed their father the next morning, he decided it must be a gift from God. He promised not to ever sell his oldest daughter into slavery.

But before long, his financial situation was as bad as before, and this time he decided to sell his second daughter. When Nicholas heard

In other versions of Nicholas's story, he threw his bag of gold through an open window of the merchant's house. North Americans' whose ancestors came from Sweden or other northern European countries may remember a tradition from their homeland—throwing Christmas gifts through an open door or window and then darting away, just as Nicholas was said to have done.

OLD WIVES' TALES

A baby born in France on Christmas is thought to have the gift of prophesy.

Daughters born on Christmas will be wise, witty, and virtuous.

what the merchant was going to do, he again went to the man's house with a bag of gold and secretly tossed it through the smoke hole. Once more, it landed in the daughters' stockings where they hung drying by the fire.

The man was grateful, and he vowed to never sell his second daughter into slavery. But a few months later he once again found himself in dire financial straits. This time he made up his mind to sell his third daughter to pay his

Today crèches are common Christmas decorations, both inside and outdoors.

A MERRY CHRISTMAS

According to legend, the historical Saint Nicholas may have tossed his gifts into a smoke hole in the chimney. By the 19th century, Santa Claus was coming down the chimney to deliver his goodies.

debts. Nicholas came to his rescue yet again—but this time, the man ran after Nicholas and caught him.

"Thank you, good sir, thank you," the merchant said, grasping Nicholas by the sleeve. "If the Lord in his compassion had not awakened your pity, my three daughters and I would have been destroyed."

After Nicholas's death, this story spread through the land where he lived. His story may be barely recognizable in today's Santa Claus, our red-garbed, jolly descendent of Saint Nicholas. But people in the fifth century came to connect Nicholas with a generosity that never gets tired of giving, with an open heart that reaches out to help without judging—and that same generous spirit lives on in today's holiday. During this holiday of good will to all, we continue to celebrate Christmas with traditions that honor the gifts of light, hope, and life.

Even our animals join the Christmas celebration.

TWO

Christmas Animals
Legends of Humility and Wonder

Santa's reindeer are some of the most familiar Christmas creatures.

Before the Wise Men began their trip, a servant was sent to the market to buy camels. One of the purchases was a mother camel who was very strong and could move quickly through the desert. But she had a newborn calf, which the owner did not mention to the servant.

When the camels were prepared to leave, the littlest camel followed his mother. No one spotted the tiny camel among the many bags and bundles, and they had been traveling for many days when he was finally noticed. But by then the baby could not be sent back.

The poor little camel had a difficult time keeping up with the caravan. Even the larger camels struggled to make their way up tall sand dunes and rocky slopes, and the little camel tripped and tumbled as he followed his mother. When they finally arrived in a town, the littlest camel hoped they would stop and rest. Instead the caravan continued through windy streets. At one point a young boy hit the littlest camel in the head with a stone and knocked him down. When he struggled back to his feet, his mother and the rest of the caravan was gone.

With dust from the road all around him, the littlest camel ran to find his mother. He found the caravan stopped in the entrance to a stable along the side of the road. Everyone, including the large camels, was kneeling. The young camel tripped and landed just inside the stable with a cry. He felt a small hand touch his forehead—and he heard a voice only his ears could hear. The childlike voice said, "You have worked so hard following your mother through the desert. As your reward you will share my blessings with all children."

From then on the littlest camel has done his part to spread the love of the Christ Child by bringing gifts to children at Christmastime.

THIS Syrian legend was brought to North America by immigrants and has been retold as a children's story. In some families, the littlest camel leaves the children their gifts instead of Santa Claus.

Ever since the earliest Christmas celebrations, people have honored the animals who played a part in the Nativity. Stories and pictures show a donkey carrying Mary on the long journey from Nazareth to Bethlehem. Camels brought the Wise Men from the east. Sheep witnessed the angels as they appeared to the shepherds. Other animals lived in the stable where the baby was born. Even the baby's crib, a manger, was a trough for feeding animals.

One popular legend tells that animals are given the gift of speech at midnight so that they may share the joy of Jesus' birth with others. Another warns that any humans who try to overhear the animals talking with one another will be punished. Yet another story says that barnyard animals show their devotion to Jesus by kneeling on the stroke of midnight on Christmas Eve. Native Americans who  converted to Christianity added their own version by sharing their belief that deer also kneel at midnight in homage to Jesus.

The average North American child today may not know about the talking, kneeling Christmas animals—but that same child will certainly know that camels and Christmas are inti-

Camels were used by merchants carrying frankincense from southern Arabia to the northern Middle East. Their ability to carry heavy loads up to almost 1,000 pounds and to travel over long distances at speeds of 25 miles a day proved advantageous in the desert. What's more these beasts are able to go about a week without food and water. They can lose 25 percent of their body weight without impairing normal functions; which may be why some tales claim that the Wise Men's camels traveled for 12 to 13 days to Bethlehem without food, water, or rest. Camels were the primary source of transportation in the desert, and for many the camel became a sign of wealth in the ancient world.

mately connected. Even frosted Christmas cookies come shaped like camels!

Sheep are also part of the Christmas story. An Arabian folktale tells this story.

MANY flocks of sheep grazed on the hills of Judea, including two late-born lambs. They loved to listen to their shepherds talking among themselves. An ancient shepherd told of a child who would be born to poor parents but would become a king. He told them that before the fulfillment of a great prophecy there would always be a sign.

British beekeepers put holly on their beehives in December to remember the bees who buzzed lullabies on Christmas Eve.

This was an exciting thought to the lambs. Shepherds were lowly, so they wondered if one of the shepherds' babies would be the king. They waited for the sign of which the shepherd spoke.

As they watched and listened, nothing happened, and finally the smaller lamb said, "One can never find anything unless you search for it. Not even grass. Let's go look for the child."

So the two small lambs began their search. First they looked into every hut and explored the fires where shepherds kept watch. But they did not find the baby. They continued along the road between the hills until they arrived at the road to Bethlehem.

As the two sheep walked, the larger lamb complained that they were foolish to keep going. He lay down to sleep.

"You stay here and sleep," said the other lamb. "But I am going to keep looking."

As the smaller lamb traveled, he searched the sky and saw a star. Suddenly, he heard the song of angels. He knew then that the star was the sign he had been seeking. So he followed it to a humble stable.

The lamb could here the lowing of cattle from inside the stable. When he entered and saw the baby and his mother, he knelt beside the child and nuzzled his tiny hands. Then he said to the baby, "You and I will remember that a small lamb was the first to find you, the Christ Child."

> Better be nice in Sweden, because naughty children get a butt from the Yul-bock (ram). Parents remind their children of the ram by placing a small straw goat among their Christmas candles. In Norway if the ram eats the food left out by the children on Christmas Eve, it means good luck. If he leaves the bowl filled with grain there will be a fine crop.

THE cow is also thought to be one of the first to witness the birth of Jesus. The Spanish believe that we should be kind to cows because their breath warmed the Baby. In Scotland, farmers feed cattle extra food on Christmas Day.

Another tale tells of a night when the baby Jesus would not sleep. His mother Mary tried in vain to calm his crying; finally, she asked the animals to help her. A tabby cat curled up by Jesus' side purring—and the restful sound soon put him to sleep. To reward the cat for his help, Mary placed an "M" on the tabby's forehead.

Birds also have their role at the Nativity. According to legend,

Robins were once thought of as Christmas birds.

a small brown bird shared Bethlehem's stable with the holy family. One night, she noticed the fire was going out, so she flew down from the rafters and fanned the fire with her wings throughout the night to keep the baby Jesus warm. In the morning, she was rewarded with a red breast as a symbol of her love for the newborn king.

Obeying another tradition, long-ago families brought their animals in the house on Christmas Eve so they could see the decorated Christmas tree. All animals were allowed in except for spiders, because housewives did not want spider webs everywhere. The spiders complained to the Christ Child, who felt sorry they had to miss the celebration. He let them in the see the trees, and the spiders became so excited they climbed all over the trees, leaving spider webs on all the branches. The Christ Child then made all the webs sparkle, and from that time on people decorated trees with "angel hair" (spun glass) to remember those beautiful webs.

*Clement C. Moore's poem, "A Visit from St. Nicholas,"
made reindeer forever a part of Christmas folklore.*

Although many of the animal legends are very old, the legend
of the reindeer is relatively recent. One story says that the Christ
Child told Saint Nicholas he could have any animal he wanted to
pull his sleigh. He chose the reindeer. But it was the poem "A
Visit from St. Nicholas" by Clement C. Moore that made reindeer
a permanent part of Santa's story.

> *'Twas the night before Christmas, when all through the house*
> *Not a creature was stirring, not even a mouse;*
> *The stockings were hung by the chimney with care,*
> *In hopes that St. Nicholas soon would be there.*
> *The children were nestled all snug in their beds,*

Santa's most famous reindeer was born in 1939, when *Rudolph the Red-Nosed Reindeer* was first written as a give-away booklet for Montgomery Ward. The author was a copywriter named Robert L. May. The booklet was given away again in 1946. May's friend, songwriter, Johnny Marks, wrote the music but they could not sell it. Finally, Marks formed his own company, St. Nicholas Music, and asked Gene Autry to sing the song. Autry agreed. "Rudolph the Red-Nosed Reindeer" became Autry's biggest hit, and Columbia Record's biggest seller ever— and today Rudolph is a part of Christmas folklore.

While visions of sugar-plums danced in their heads;
And mamma in her 'kerchief, and I in my cap,
Had just settled down for a long winter's nap,
When out on the lawn there arose such a clatter,
I sprang from the bed to see what was the matter.
Away to the window I flew like a flash,

In the 19th century, people imagined horses pulling Santa's sleigh rather than reindeer.

Today Heifer Project International is an organization that allows animals to play a role in Christmas by providing livestock to needy families around the world. A group or an individual can purchase sheep, dairy cows, goats, ducks, honeybees, camels, llamas, and more. By doing so they provide a Christmas gift that keeps on giving in the form of milk or eggs; valuable draft animals for hauling loads; fertilizer; and income from the sale of any extra dairy products, honey, wool, or offspring. The program requires that recipients give one of their animal's female offspring to another family in their community.

Tore open the shutters and threw up the sash.
The moon on the breast of the new-fallen snow,
Gave the luster of mid-day to objects below,
When, what to my wondering eyes should appear,
But a miniature sleigh, and eight tiny reindeer,
With a little old driver, so lively and quick,
I knew in a moment it must be St. Nick.
More rapid than eagles his coursers they came,
And he whistled, and shouted, and called them by name;
"Now, DASHER! now, DANCER! now, PRANCER and VIXEN!
On, COMET! on CUPID! on, DONNER and BLITZEN!
To the top of the porch! to the top of the wall!
Now dash away! dash away! dash away all!"
As dry leaves that before the wild hurricane fly,
When they meet with an obstacle, mount to the sky,

Today, we connect eggs with Easter—but 19th-century greeting cards used the egg as symbol of hope at Christmas time as well.

So up to the house-top the coursers they flew,
With the sleigh full of toys, and St. Nicholas too.
And then, in a twinkling, I heard on the roof
The prancing and pawing of each little hoof.

Ever since the first Christmas, animals have been associated with Christmas.

Christmas is not for the rich and important. Instead, according to tradition, Christmas is a gift of joy and light and hope for the earth's most simple and humble creatures. Perhaps it is no wonder then that animals are such a large part of Christmas folklore. Animals have yielded food, clothing, and labor to humans throughout history. Without them, human lives would not be the same; our lives are knit together with theirs.

Christmas folklore is full of symbols of hope—and that hope is extended to the entire earth, including the beasts.

In our current world, gift-giving is one of the most important Christmas traditions.

THREE

The Wise Men
The First Gift-Givers

Across North America, no Christmas morning would be complete without packages to open.

AFTER JESUS was born in Bethlehem in Judea, during the time of King Herod, Magi from the east came to Jerusalem and asked, "Where is the one who has been born king of the Jews? We saw his star in the east and have come to worship him...they went on their way, and the star they had seen in the east went ahead of them until it stopped over the place where the child was. When they saw the star, they were overjoyed. On coming to the house, they saw the child with his mother Mary, and they bowed down and worshiped him. Then they opened their treasures and presented him with gifts of gold and of incense and of myrrh. (Matthew 2:1–2, 9–11)

THE Wise Men probably arrived in Bethlehem from somewhere near the present-day land of Iran. They were ancient scholars of **astrology**, and they were considered to be knowledgeable and wise. According to tradition, there were *three* Wise Men, but the only evidence of this in the Bible story is the statement that there were three gifts: gold, *myrrh*, and **frankincense**.

Guided by a bright star, the Wise Men (or Magi) traveled a great distance. They made a long journey to present their gifts to the King of the Jews—and yet they were not Jews themselves. Legend tells that when the kings returned to their homes, they shared their wealth with those in need and became preachers of the gospel of Christ. According to folklore accounts, they met the apostle Thomas about 40 years later in India. He baptized them and ordained them as priests. Eventually they were **martyred** for their faith in Christ.

January 6, Epiphany, is the holiday that remembers the Wise

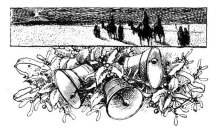

Men's discovery of the Christ Child. Many celebrate this as the end of the Christmas season. In New Orleans, families traditionally gather together during this season. After the Christmas Eve midnight mass, a celebration begins which marks the wanderings of the Three Wise Men. These festivities end on January 6, the day the Wise Men ended their journey.

The Wise Men show up in the folklore of cultures around the world, as this Italian folktale illustrates.

ONCE, an old woman known as La Befana lived in a little village. She was too busy keeping her little house and yard spotless to be friendly with her neighbors. Because of her endless sweeping, the old woman spent much of her time making brooms.

One morning La Befana was up early sweeping when she heard a knock on the door. She wondered why anyone would interrupt her cleaning. The old woman opened the door only a

THE CHRISTMAS STAR

The stars that hang in churches and on Christmas trees during the Christmas season represent the star that led the Wise Men to the Christ Child. Even the stars cut from cookie dough remind us of the light that guides us through the Christmas season.

English monarchs set out boxes in which their subjects were to give Christmas gifts to them. The gifts were classified according to rank and means; even the poorest subject was required to give something to the reigning monarch. Queen Elizabeth I replenished her wardrobe each year with the more generous gifts from her wealthier subjects. Furs, jewels, petticoats, and silk stockings were among her Christmas tokens.

Brightly wrapped presents express our love to one another.

Lighting luminaries to line walkways is a Christmas tradition that calls to mind the Wise Men, travelers whose way was lit by divine light.

In England, the day after Christmas is called Boxing Day. On this day people would box up food and clothing and give to folks who couldn't afford gifts for themselves and others.

crack, but she was so amazed by what she saw that she flung the door wide. Standing before her were not one, not two, but three kings. She had never seen even a single king before, but she knew by their beautiful robes that these men were indeed kings.

"We are lost," one king said. "We are looking for the baby who was born in Bethlehem. A star shone in the East and we followed it to offer our gifts to the child who will be King."

La Befana had heard of this prophesy also but she knew nothing about the baby's whereabouts, for she rarely left her home. "I cannot help you," she said.

"We must continue to search," another king spoke. "Will you come with us?"

Leave? Before the day's sweeping was finished? She couldn't. La Befana shook her head. She stood in the doorway as the wise men moved out of sight.

Although La Befana continued sweeping, the work did not seem the same. She no longer cared about the dust. Why hadn't she gone with the kings to visit the baby? She could think of nothing else all day long. The next morning she started out, trying to catch up with her visitors.

She never found the kings. She never reached Bethlehem, and she never saw the baby.

Travelers who leave gifts are common in Christmas folklore. Today's gift-giver is said to travel by sleigh.

But all along her journey she stopped at the homes of children, leaving gifts in hopes that some day she would find the young baby.

OUR Santa Claus folklore and other Christmas traditions have been shaped by centuries-old stories like this one. Even the tradition of giving gifts is rooted in the Saturnalia celebration in ancient Rome. Other ancient gift-givers include Odin, a Norse god who rode an eight-footed horse named Slepnir. Also there was the German goddess, Hertha, who was believed to bring health and good fortune  on December 25th. How did she deliver these gifts? By coming down the chimney, of course. When Hertha appeared in their fireplace, people believed she brought good luck. (Was Santa Claus originally a woman?)

The earliest Christmas gifts were the offerings of the Wise Men to the baby Jesus. Today, our jolly Saint Nick continues the tradition on his Christmas Eve sleigh ride. But the spirit of generosity and open-heartedness is the same.

Santa Claus has been imagined in many different ways over the centuries. The one thing that holds true down through the years is this: Santa brings gifts!

FOUR

Santa Claus
The Saint of Generosity

Children's belief in Santa Claus is a vital part of family Christmas traditions.

SANTA CLAUS HAS experienced many changes throughout the years of his benevolent giving. He is known in many
countries by different names, but his mission is closely linked
with that of the Wise Men: he is the giver of gifts and joy. Although children are the most apparent recipients of his yuletide
treasures, Santa's kindhearted generosity has influenced young
and old alike for centuries.

Saint Nicholas is the Catholic **patron saint** of boys and girls.
As a patron saint, Saint Nicholas is believed to care for children
all over the world as they pray and ask for his guidance. But it is
his generous nature that won him a place in the hearts of people
everywhere as the bearer of gifts to those who do good throughout the year.

As we mentioned in chapter one, Nicholas was a real man
who lived during the fifth century as a bishop of the Christian
church in a town called Myra located in Asia Minor. He was a
kind, generous, and courageous example to those around him.
One of the legends about Nicholas tells that on the day he was
born he stood up and clasped his hands, raised his eyes toward
heaven, and gave thanks to God for having created him. He was
also said to refuse milk until after sundown on Wednesdays and
Fridays, both days of fasting for the church. His parents were
very wealthy, and although they died when he was quite young,
he had provisions enough for an affluent life—but Saint Nicholas
chose to give away his money to the poor and to the church.

According to another legend, Nicholas sailed to the Holy
Land to visit the tomb of Jesus Christ, but the ship was caught in

Although Santa has traditionally worn a red robe, in the 19th century, he was often portrayed in white.

a terrible storm. The captain and his crew had given up hope for their safe arrival, when Nicholas prayed that the wind and waves would calm down. The ship was saved.

He was once said to have made the sign of the cross over a badly burned child, who was instantly restored to health. After his death, he miraculously brought a lost boy home to his parents. Sailors and merchants carried stories of his power to Italy, and they spread from there throughout Europe.

At the beginning of the 12th century, nuns from some of the convents in central France

Saint Nicholas was the youngest bishop in the history of the Roman Catholic Church. Many churches throughout Europe have been dedicated to him.

began leaving gifts secretly at the houses of poor families on Saint Nicholas Eve, December 5. The gifts consisted of good things to eat, like fruits and nuts and even oranges from Spain.

The custom spread throughout Europe; the Dutch celebrated Saint Nicholas Day on December 6, and their traditions laid the foundation for our modern Christmas season. Dutch children placed their wooden shoes beside the fireplace before they went to bed. Sinterklaas, as he was called in Dutch, rode a white horse and wore the bishop's fur-trimmed red robe and traditional **mitered** hat. He and his helper, Black Peter,

Today's jolly saint was once a Catholic bishop.

In the 1890s, an artist named Thomas Nast used drawings like this one to create our modern image of Santa as a chubby, jovial fellow.

stopped at each house to fill the shoes of good boys and girls with small presents, cakes, and candies. Sinterklaas was also known to smoke a pipe.

In the 16th century, German children believed in Krist Kindle, the Christ Child, who brought gifts on Christmas Eve. Martin Luther was responsible for this belief, because he felt that Saint Nicolas was leading everyone away from the true meaning of Christmas. According to the tradition he initiated, gifts were brought to the children by Christ's messenger, a young girl with a golden crown. Today, however, Krist Kindle has evolved into Chris Cringle, another name for Santa Claus.

STOCKING HANGING

In 1809, while writing the *Knickerbocker History of New York*, Washington Irving told of hanging stockings on Saint Nichols Eve, the first mention in print of this custom.

In 1835, President Andrew Jackson's niece Mary Donelson and several other children hung their stockings from the mantel in the President's room. The children talked him into hanging a stocking too. The children received gifts of silver quarters, cakes, nuts, candy, fruit, and toys. The President received a pair of slippers, a cob pipe, and a tobacco bag.

The Santa Claus who comes down the chimney bearing gifts grew from a long history of story and tradition.

This most popular letter and editorial first appeared in the *New York Sun* in 1897. The *Sun* continued to reprint the letter every Christmas until 1949 when the paper went out of business.

"Is there a Santa Claus?"

We take pleasure in answering thus prominently the communication below, expressing at the same time our great gratification that its faithful author is numbered among the friends of *The Sun*:

Dear Editor—
I am 8 years old. Some of my little friends say there is no Santa Claus. Papa says, "If you see it in The Sun, it's so." Please tell me the truth, is there a Santa Claus?
—Virginia O'Hanlon, 115 West Ninety-fifth Street

Virginia, your little friends are wrong. They have been affected by the skepticism of a sceptical age. They do not believe except they see. They think that nothing can be which is not comprehensible by their little minds. All minds, Virginia, whether they be men's or children's, are little. In this great universe of ours, man is a mere insect, an ant, in his intellect as compared with the boundless world about him, as measured by the intelligence capable of grasping the whole truth and knowledge.

Yes, Virginia there is a Santa Claus He exists as certainly as love and generosity and devotion exist, and you know that they abound and give to your life its highest beauty and joy. Alas! How dreary would be the world if there were no Santa Claus! It would be as dreary as if there were no Virginias. There would be no childlike faith then, no poetry, no romance to make tolerable this existence. We should have no enjoyment, except in sense and sight. The external light with which childhood fills the world would be extinguished.

Not believe in Santa Claus! You might as well not believe in fairies. You might get your papa to have men to watch in all the chimneys on Christmas eve to catch Santa

Claus, but even if you did not see Santa Claus coming down, what would that prove? Nobody sees Santa Claus, but that is no sign that there is no Santa Claus. The most real things in the world are those that neither children nor men can see. Did you ever see fairies dancing on the lawn? Of course not, but that's no proof that they are not there. Nobody can conceive or imagine all the wonders there are unseen and unseeable in the world.

You tear apart the baby's rattle and see what makes the noise inside, but there is a veil covering the unseen world which not the strongest man, nor even the united strength of all the strongest men that ever lived could tear apart. Only faith, poetry, love romance, can push aside that curtain and view and picture the supernal beauty and glory beyond. Is it all real? Ah, Virginia, in all this world there is nothing else real and abiding.

For Swedish children, Jultomten is the one who brings gifts in a sleigh pulled by the goats of the thunder god, Thor. In Ghana, Africa, Father Christmas comes from the jungle to deliver his gifts. In Hawaii, he rides in a boat. But more for most of the United States and Canada, he is Santa Claus, and he drives a sleigh full of toys pulled by eight reindeer.

DEAR Santa
these are For you
I HAVE BEEN a VERY
good girl all year
EXCEPT to my brother
But thats O.K
are Bou

A popular American tradition is the leaving of milk and cookies for the Christmas Eve visitor. In the morning children wake to an empty glass and only crumbs on the plate . . . proof that Santa has been there.

One of the most recent legends of Santa Claus is about his workshop located at the North Pole. There Santa, Mrs. Claus, the elves, and the reindeer live all year preparing for the Christmas Eve flight of the jolly gift-giver. Eight tiny reindeer pull a sleigh filled with toys requested by children all over the world. Santa lands on the rooftops and slides down chimneys to deliver the treasures into stockings and under brightly decorated Christmas trees.

Frosty the Snowman is a 20th-century Christmas legend. Although he's not as popular as Santa—after all Frosty doesn't bring gifts—Frosty's fame has grown beyond his song. Today he's a prominent figure in Christmas decorations across North America.

Early 20th-century Christmas music added to Santa's fame.

Wonderful tales have evolved from this myth, and filmmakers and television producers have taken every liberty to produce elaborate sets with views of reindeer barns, Santa's workshop, and streets lined with candy canes and lights. This, too, is a gift of imagination and celebration that encourages the spirit of the season.

Today Santa Claus' benevolent nature continues to inspire young and old to mimic his celebration of gift giving.

Today the Christmas tree is one of the central symbols of Christmas.

FIVE

Christmas Greens
and Flowers
Symbols of Everlasting Life

The Christmas tree may be rooted in pagan customs, but in the 19th century, it began to be the focus of Christmas's gift-giving traditions.

ALONG TIME AGO Boniface, an English monk who helped to organize the church in France and Germany, was walking through the woods. He met a group of people who worshipped the god Thor. They had with them a child who was to be sacrificed as part of their worship.

The people were gathered around a large oak tree that was sacred to them. Because the oak tree was considered a god, the worship ceremony took place at its trunk. So much did Boniface want to save the child that he cut down the huge tree with one mighty blow. The tree split into four pieces, and from its center grew an evergreen tree. Boniface told the people that their god was dead and the fir tree was the tree of Christ, the giver of eternal life.

Throughout history, Christmas greens have symbolized life. Romans decorated their homes with palm branches and evergreens to celebrate the Saturnalia festival. The ancient Romans not only decorated their homes but they gave one another green branches for good luck.

CHRISTMAS TREES

The first Christmas tree decorated during the Middle Ages was called the "Paradise Tree." Apples and small wafer cookies adorned the evergreen. The trees were then used in **mummers'** plays and in homes to help tell the story of Adam and Eve.

Martin Luther is said to have started the tradition of decorating a pine tree for Christmas. He had been traveling and was returning through the woods to his home. Anxious to be with his family for the holiday, he looked up at the clear sky and shining stars. Noticing how beautiful the stars looked twinkling between the evergreen tree branches, he was reminded of what the sky must have been like in Bethlehem on the night Jesus was born. He wanted to share this beauty with his family, so on impulse, he cut down a tree and took it into his house. Placing candles on the branches, Luther called his wife and children to gather around the tree and remember the Christ Child.

The earliest written description of decorating a tree is from 1605 when a traveler wrote about a tree in Strasbourg, in Alsace, decorated with cookies and candies.

As decorating the Christmas tree became more popular, small gifts appeared on its branches. Pinecones, cookies, fruit, and nuts made the trees more festive. Candles brightened the branches. In the 1840s, Queen Victoria and Prince Albert of England adopted the tree-trimming ritual. They added miniature toys and animals, baskets, and paper *cornucopias* filled with candy.

As people from Germany moved to North America, they brought the Christmas tree tradition with them. Some trees were decorated with carved wooden figures. These animals, stars, and other symbols were sometimes too heavy for the tree branches, and people searched for lighter decorations. The first hand-blown ornaments were produced during the latter half of the 19th century in Germany by individuals who worked from their own homes. They supplied the growing ornament industry with delicate glass balls of various colors and shapes. Before long,

Tinsel was first used in Germany in 1610. The thin strips of silver foil made in Nuremberg, Germany, became very popular in the United States. Because they tarnished quickly over the years, manufacturers tried making them from lead foil, which posed a threat of lead poisoning; finally, in the 1960s, tinsel was made from mylar plastic.

Immigrants from Germany brought the Christmas tree tradition with them to the New World.

glassblowing became the occupation of whole German towns, like Lauscha, where beautiful ornaments were made totally by hand and sent to America to sell.

One folktale tells that when Christ was born, all the creatures on earth, including the trees, went to Bethlehem to give him

gifts. Those trees that were fruit bearing gave from their harvest—but the fir tree had nothing to give. An angel felt sorry for the tree, and asked some stars to sit on the tree's branches. The legend says that when Jesus saw the tree, shining and beautiful, he blessed it . . . and so the custom of decorating trees with ornaments began.

In the 19th century, the first Christmas angel was introduced for the top of Christmas trees. Most trees also included a "Christmas yard" that held miniature people and animals surrounded by a fence. These were placed beneath the tree's branches; although it is not clear why the fences were used, they remained popular for many years. By the 1940s and 1950s, electric trains became a popular gift and the yards once surrounding trees became train layouts with villages, train cars that loaded lumber or milk tins, and tiny trees or other landscaping.

Once trees became a part of North American tradition, the White House occupants began to take part. President Andrew

The first electrically lighted tree was lit in the home of Edward Johnson in 1882. He was a colleague of Thomas Edison.

Christmas trees are grown across North America.

Jackson was especially fond of Christmas. In 1835, his chef made him a sugar-frosted pine tree with iced toy animals surrounding it. Several decades later, in 1856, Franklin Pierce set up the first decorated Christmas tree in the White House.

In 1895, Grover Cleveland used the first electric lights on the White House tree. But a few years later, in 1902, Theodore Roosevelt would not let his children have a Christmas tree. He was a **conservationist**, and he feared that the Christmas tree industry would ruin the forests. His friend, Gifford Pinchot, the chief United States Forester,

About one million acres of land are planted with Christmas trees. Eighteen people receive their daily oxygen from only one acre of trees.

For many families, picking out the perfect Christmas tree is an essential part of Christmas.

finally convinced him that cutting smaller trees helped the larger trees grow better.

According to yet another tradition, though, Archibald Roosevelt, Teddy's young son, was the one who changed the President's mind. Archibald purchased a 20-cent tree and stowed it in a closet in the room where his parents had hidden the Christmas presents. Decorated with tiny lights and presents for his parents, the hidden tree was revealed on Christmas morning. His special treat is said to have changed his father's mind forever.

HOLLY

Because holly was an evergreen, the ancient Celts thought it was a holy tree. They believed that the sun, their god, had rewarded the holly for its goodness by allowing it to remain green all year. Sacred things were thought to have spirits living in them, so when the Celts brought the holly indoors to decorate their homes, they were sheltering the good spirits from winter's hardships.

The sacred plant of the god Saturn, holly was also used in many of the Saturnalia celebrations. Wreaths were made and worn by the Romans, and people even gave them to one another as gifts. Images of Saturn were decorated with holly leaves.

These holly-trimmed images may have been another forerunner of our Santa Claus. When the Romans occupied England in AD 43, they brought with them their Saturnalia celebrations.

The holly wreath on Santa's head connects him to Saturn, the ancient Romans' god.

After they left, the English adapted the Roman celebrations and merged them with their own. The echoes of many of these traditions can still be heard in English Christmas celebrations. For instance, the English thought of Father Christmas as a huge man dressed in a scarlet robe lined with fur. Like Saturn, on his head, he wore a crown of holly—and like Saturn, he was a symbol of feasting, drinking, and merriment.

The Christmas colors of red and green come from the plants that live throughout the winter, evergreen trees and holly berries.

According to Christian folk beliefs, the holly's white flowers symbolize Christ's purity, the red berries his blood; the leaves represent the crown of thorns he wore on the cross, and the bitter bark the sorrow he bore.

MISTLETOE

A Norse myth tells that Balder, the sun god, dreamed of his own death. His mother, Frigga, the goddess of love, was so scared by the dream that she went to air, fire, water, earth, the animals, and the plants, begging them to promise not to do anything to hurt her son. Somehow, she forgot to ask the mistletoe. Maybe she missed it because mistletoe, instead of growing on its own, grew on the oak and apple trees as a parasite, receiving its nourishment from the host tree.

Loki, god of evil, was jealous of Balder. When he heard of Balder's dream, he decided this was his chance to get his enemy. So he thought of a plan and made an arrow tip from some mistletoe and gave it to Hoder, the blind god of winter. Without realizing what he was doing, Hoder shot and killed Balder, the god of light.

At his death, the sky began to darken. The other gods were so sad they each took turns trying to bring Balder back to life. Finally, his mother Frigga, through her love for him, was able to succeed. Her tears turned into the berries on the mistletoe plant. She was so happy to have her son alive again that she kissed each god who walked under the tree where the mistletoe grew. From then on, she

One superstition says that if a girl refuses to be kissed while under the mistletoe she should not expect to get married during the following year.

said the mistletoe would never hurt anyone again . . . and anyone standing underneath the plant would get kissed as an expression of love.

In the Celtic world, mistletoe was a symbol of immortality, strength, and physical healing. It played an important part in Celts' New Year rituals at the beginning of November, denoting the passing from one life to another higher life.

Centuries after the ancient Celts, kisses were exchanged in England beneath mistletoe as the ceremonial ending of a grievance. Sprigs of mistletoe were hung over doors for the same reason, as a way of saying that the hosts wished peace to all their guests. Today mistletoe symbolizes joy. And couples still kiss beneath its branches.

POINSETTIA

In 1828, Dr. Joel Roberts Poinsett discovered flowering red plants while in Mexico. He sent some cuttings to a nurseryman, Robert Buist, in Philadelphia. Buist later named the plant Poinsettia *pulcherrima*. The Mexicans called the flower the Flor de la Noche Buena (Flower of the Holy Night.)

Mexican legend says that the poinsettia originated from a miracle. A poor child who went to visit Jesus had nothing to bring as a gift, so he gathered weeds and made a small bouquet. As the little boy approached the Christ Child, the weeds were transformed into brilliant red blooms.

Today the poinsettia is the most traditional of all flowering Christmas plants. But it was not until 1963 that a strain was developed with the

Poinsettias' "blossoms" are actually colored leaves.

ability to live outside a greenhouse as well as keep its blooms for an extended period. So although it has become extremely popular, it is a relative newcomer in Christmas tradition.

THE CHRISTMAS ROSE

One of the many legends surrounding the Christmas rose tells a story of a country girl named Madelon who spoke with the shepherds on their way to Bethlehem. The Wise Men, bearing their gifts, also passed by the field where she tended her sheep. Each

By the early 20th century, poinsettias had replaced roses as a Christmas flower.

told her of the baby they were seeking. They showed her wonderful gifts they were bringing to Jesus. When they had continued their journey toward the manger, Madelon began to cry. An angel that saw her tears and asked why she wept.

"I have nothing to bring the baby," she said.

The angel waved his hand . . . and the pathway to Bethlehem was instantly lined with beautiful white roses. Gathering an armful, Madelon rushed to the manger, where Mary motioned her to come to Jesus. Madelon knelt beside the Christ Child and shared her gift with him.

The Christmas rose blooms during the winter. When the rest of the earth is barren and cold, the rose is a sign of life and hope.

ROSEMARY

Rosemary is believed to have received its smell when Mary hung Jesus' baby blankets over it to dry. Its beautiful gray-green color is said to have come from her cloak hanging on its branches. Today it is used mainly as a spice, but rosemary is also desired for its good smell.

The Christmas wreath's circle is a symbol of eternity.

I bring you CHRISTMAS GREETINGS.

Mistletoe, an evergreen, was a common Christmas image on early holiday postcards.

At a time of the year when much of the northern hemisphere is cold and barren, the evergreen branches and blooming flowers bring welcome color into our lives. Although we no longer believe we need to bring evergreens in for fear of the sun not returning, we still enjoy the sight and smell of live greens and flowers in our homes. They are a statement of hope and faith.

Christmas joy is in my heart

In many countries, like Poland, straw is scattered around the house on Christmas Eve. The family then eats dinner on a cloth spread on the floor, almost like a winter picnic. As they eat they remember that the Baby Jesus was born in a manger and that he had only straw for a bed.

The holiday's themes of hospitality and plenty are symbolized by food.

SIX

Christmas Food
Traditions of Hospitality
and Plenty

We connect particular dishes with Christmas.

CANDY CANES, cookies, eggnog, fruitcake, lollypops, and . . . visions of sugarplums dancing in their heads!

When we think of Christmas we remember wonderful baked goods; we call to mind Christmas meals that included good food, laughter, friends, and family. Food feeds both our bodies and our souls. It offers us wonderful memories and special times, fulfilling our need for nourishment and companionship. Throughout human history, whenever there has been a reason to celebrate, there has also been a reason to eat and be thankful.

Years ago, food was still a large part of the Christmas tradition. Even the poorest people prepared the largest holiday fare they could. Many families ate the fattened pig for Christmas dinner. The average person was happy with a joint of pork or a cured ham for their special dinner. Menu choices were as simple as a turkey, potatoes, and gravy—or as elaborate as venison, peacock, swan, beef, and **capon**.

King Henry VIII, King of England, named wild boar as the official dish of Christmas. The boar's head was brought by the chef to the feast table on a gold platter garnished with rosemary and laurel. In the mouth of the boar was a lemon or an apple. Servants following the chef sang as the platter was brought in procession, and a special man who was said to have virtue and courage was chosen to carve the boar.

One legend tells of a student from Queen's College, Oxford, who was surprised by an attacking wild boar as he walked through the forest reading Aristotle. Having no time to draw his sword, the scholar jammed his book into the boar's mouth and choked him to death. Happy with his conquest, he cut off the boar's head and carried it back to the college. It was then roasted and served with much ceremony. The tradition of the roasted Christmas boar's head continued there and elsewhere for years to come.

Today, giving food as gifts is popular during the Christmas season. Simple foods like a loaf of homemade bread, jar of preserves, or dish of decorated cookies are popular offerings. Many give chocolates or hard candies, oranges and grapefruits, and nuts of all kinds.

One of the most well-known gifts of food was the large Christmas turkey given to Bob Cratchit and his family by the newly transformed Scrooge in Dickens' *A Christmas Carol*.

In the story, Scrooge yells down into the street to a boy in his Sunday clothes.

LETTING IN CHRISTMAS

Christmas and hospitality have always gone hand in hand. There is a belief that the first guest to enter a house on Christmas Day can bring the dwellers good luck throughout the year. The person's sex and hair color play an important part in this belief, for gook luck it should be a dark-haired man carrying a sprig of ever-green. He should enter through the front door and exit through the back door. He must not have red hair and he must not be a she—or look out for disaster.

"Do you know whether they have sold the prize turkey that was hanging up there? Not the little prize turkey: the big one?"

"What the one as big as me?" returned the boy.

"What a delightful boy!" said Scrooge. "It's a pleasure to talk to him. Yes, my buck!"

"It's hanging there now," replied the boy.

"Is it?" said Scrooge. "Go and buy it."

"Walk-ER!" exclaimed the boy.

"No, no," said Scrooge, "I am in earnest. Go and buy it, and tell 'em to bring it here, that I may give them the direction where to take it. . . I'll send it to Bob Cratchit's!" whispered Scrooge, rubbing his hands, and splitting with a laugh. "He shan't know who sends it. It's twice the size of Tiny Tim."

The gift of food for the Cratchits meant hospitality, happiness, and celebration. Food is the gift that seems to break the barriers between us. A good meal helps us forget our differences. And in many homes along with the Christmas feast comes fun. Games, dancing, and conversation warm the heart and allow us to forget the work that we must go back to all too soon. For now hospitality reigns, just as it did in this tale from colonial New York State.

A long time ago in the Dutch colony of Albany, New York, an honest baker named Van Amsterdam opened a small bakeshop. Each morning he balanced his scales so he could give his customers exactly what they paid for, no more or no less.

Every year on December 6, when the colony celebrated Saint Nicholas Day, Van Amsterdam made the most wonderful cut-out cookies. Each was made from gingerbread in the likeness of Saint

Nicholas and iced in red and white, with the high red bishop's cap and the long red bishop's cloak.

One morning a woman entered the shop just as the baker was ready to open for business. The elderly woman asked Van Amsterdam for a dozen Saint Nicholas cookies.

The baker carefully counted 12 cookies and began packaging them.

"You only gave me 12 cookies," the woman said.

"That is right," Van Amsterdam said. "You asked for a dozen cookies—and 12 is a dozen."

The elderly woman insisted that a dozen was 13; she wanted him to give her one more cookie.

But Van Amsterdam insisted that he was a fair man and always gave everyone exactly what they paid for, no more or no less.

"Keep your cookies," the woman said as she left his shop. Then she turned back toward the baker, "You may be honest but your heart is small. You have a lot to learn."

The elderly woman disappeared, but from

> Eating apples at midnight on Christmas Eve meant you would enjoy good health the next year.

that day on Van Amsterdam's bakery was not the same. His bread did not raise, his pies were too tart, and his cakes fell apart. His customers were no longer happy with his baking. They shopped at other bakeries and soon Van Amsterdam had no business.

"That old woman cast a spell on my bakery," he moaned to himself. "Why is this happening to me? I am such an honest man. I deserve better."

By the next Saint Nicholas Day, Van Amsterdam had no customers and he was very poor. As he looked at his beautifully dec-

A table set for a holiday dinner communicates welcome and joy.

orated cookies, he wished that Saint Nicholas could help him. Sadly, he went to bed.

That night he dreamed he was a young boy again. He was with a crowd of children who were being offered gifts from Saint Nicholas. Van Amsterdam noticed that no matter how many offerings the saint passed out, there were always more. His white horse held the gift baskets that bulged more and more as each child received his or her present.

Nicholas reached out to hand the young Van Amsterdam his gift. It was a cookie, just like those Van Amsterdam made in his bakery.

A loaf of bread left on the table after Christmas Eve dinner meant there would be plenty of bread during the rest of the year.

When the boy looked up to thank the kindly saint, he was gone. Instead, there stood the elderly woman, smiling down on him.

When Van Amsterdam woke up, he said to himself, "Instead of giving my customers exactly what they pay for, I am going to give them a little more."

He began mixing the gingerbread dough, then cut the shapes, baked them, and iced them to look like the kindly Saint Nicholas of his dream. Just as he finished, the elderly woman walked into his shop. "May I have a dozen Saint Nicholas cookies?"

Van Amsterdam carefully counted 12 cookies and one more.

"Here you are, 13 cookies. From now on, in my shop a dozen is 13."

"You count well," the woman said. "I'm sure you will be rewarded."

As she left the store, the baker thought he saw the tail end of Saint Nicholas's long red cloak. He ran to the door but no one was there.

Van Amsterdam was rewarded. As everyone heard of his generosity, the baker enjoyed more customers than ever. Soon other bakers began giving 13 cookies as a dozen also—and that is how 13 became the "baker's dozen."

TODAY, cookie baking continues to be an important Christmas tradition. One of the wonderful gifts of cookie baking is the opportunity to share the event within the household or even several households. Grandma, Mom, the grandchildren, and Dad join in on the flour-flying, sugar-licking, and batter-beating fun.

According to one European custom, on Christmas Eve, when children went to bed, they left bread baskets or plates on the kitchen table. In the morning gifts of food were found. The Christ Child was believed to come through the keyhole during the night to deliver these gifts. This custom was known as "setting the Christ plates."

Making Christmas cookies is a favorite tradition for many families.

The finished product is then shared with friends, family, and neighbors.

Besides being delectable treats, cookies have traditionally served as decorations as well. Decorated cookies hanging from trees are recorded in many long-ago descriptions of the holiday. Other edible treats are also used as decorations, like small paper cornucopias filled with candy treats and sometimes fruits. Dried apples and  pretzels have also been used as decorations, and popcorn strings draped around the family tree offered another opportunity for

PFEFFERNUSSE
(GERMAN PEPPERNUTS)

3 cups of flour
1 tsp cinnamon
$\frac{1}{8}$ tsp cloves
$\frac{1}{3}$ cup blanched almonds, finely chopped
$\frac{1}{3}$ cup candied orange peel, finely chopped
$\frac{1}{4}$ tsp white pepper
3 eggs
1 cup sugar
powdered sugar

Combine ingredients (except for powdered sugar) and refrigerate two to three days. Roll out dough a little at a time to $\frac{1}{4}$ to $\frac{1}{2}$ inch thick. Cut dough with $1\frac{3}{4}$-inch round cookie cutter and place on greased cookie sheet, an inch apart. Bake at 350°F for 15 to 18 minutes. Store in a covered container for one to two weeks with half an apple. Before serving, roll in powdered sugar. Makes about $3\frac{1}{2}$ dozen cookies.

family fun. Children stringing popcorn, eating it, and many times throwing it at each other is a fond remembrance in many families.

From countries everywhere have come some of North America's special recipes. From Germany came the hard spicy pfeffernusse cookies called peppernuts, as well as gingerbread men. Some housewives make a German stollen cookie filled with cur-

rents and sprinkled with sugar; originally they were shaped like a manger, in honor of the Baby Jesus. The French brought cookies of whole wheat, brown sugar, and dates for the holiday. Almond paste cookies from Portugal celebrate Epiphany, the visit of the Wise Men.

In recent years, cookie exchanges have become popular. At these gatherings, people meet to enjoy each other's company and usually some Christmas festivities. Guests bring cookies to fill a community tray for the exchange; the group then takes home the leftovers or distributes them to the poor or elderly. Carolers have also long enjoyed Christmas cookies as they call on houses to share their Christmas songs. In North America probably few holiday gatherings take place that do not include the traditional Christmas cookies.

Plum pudding is another tasty traditional Christmas food, one that shows up often in stories, poems, and songs. Today it is not popular in North America, but no English Christmas was complete without it. A story tells of an English king who was forced to spend Christmas Eve in the forest. His cook stirred together all the food he brought with him, which included chopped meat, flour, apples, dried plums, eggs, ale, sugar, and brandy. The cook put the mix into a bag and boiled it. He had prepared the first Christmas plum pudding.

> Plum pudding is not made from plums—or not as we think of plums today. Most plum puddings include meat broth, raisins or dried prunes, wine, spices, and suet.

Wassail got its name from the greeting *Was haile*, which meant "Be of good health." This English greeting became associated with the custom of drinking a toast—a wassail. Toasting and

THE WASSAIL SONG

Here we come a-wassailing
Among the leaves so green,
Here we come a-wandering,
So fair to be seen.

Love and joy come to you,
And to you're your wassail too,
And God bless you, and send you
A happy new year.

drinking to each other's health was common among the poorest friends and families as well as the wealthiest and most powerful. The wassail drink was made from hot ale spiced with nutmeg, cloves, and ginger.

From this customary greeting grew the custom of wassailing, where carolers went from house to house singing. As they visited each family, they were offered a cup of wassail. The "Wassailing Song" describes this fun tradition that led to the modern tradition of Christmas caroling.

For many years food may have been the only way Christmas was celebrated, especially for many religious groups who wanted to remember the birth of Jesus without making the holiday into a "pagan" celebration. Even today, those who seek to escape the commercialism of the modern Christmas season do not disown traditional foods or meals.

Throughout the ages, many people celebrated Christmas as a

In medieval England, Christmas feasting lasted for 12 days. Kings and bishops tried to outdo each other in terms of elaborate meals. One Christmas pie was nine feet in diameter, weighed 165 pounds, and contained two bushels of flour, 20 pounds of butter, four geese, two rabbits, foul wild ducks, two woodcocks, six snipes, four partridges, two neats' tongues, two curlews, six pigeons, and seven blackbirds. In the 13th century, King Henry III butchered 600 oxen for his Christmas feast!

In English celebrations, Santa Claus—or Father Christmas—had his own part to play in the feasting. In one mummers' play, "Father Christmas" had these lines to say:

> *Here comes I, Father Christmas am I,*
> *Welcome—or welcome not;*
> *I hope old Father Christmas is never forgot. . . .*
> *Christmas comes but once a year,*
> *When it comes it brings good cheer. . . .*
> *Roast beef, plum pudding, and mince pie,*
> *Who likes them better than I?*

In the New World, as Dutch and English colonists inter-married and blended their traditions, Sinterklaas and Father Christmas blended together. By the Revolutionary War in 1783 he had a new name: Santa Claus.

FRENCH CHRISTMAS COOKIES

Christmas cookies are an important holiday food tradition. Here's a recipe for a traditional French cookie that can be decorated however you want.

½ cup butter or other softened shortening
¾ cup sugar
½ cup honey
2 egg yolks
¼ cup milk
1 tsp vanilla
3 cups flour

Cream butter and sugar together until light. Add honey and egg yolks, beating well. Next add the milk and vanilla and beat some more. Add the flour in small amounts until well blended. Chill dough for 2 hours, so that you can handle it without it being sticky. Roll ⅛″ to ¼″ thick on a lightly floured surface. Cut into whatever shapes you want and decorate with colored sugars (or wait until cookies have baked and cooled and then decorate with icing). Bake on ungreased cookie sheets for 10 minutes at 375 degrees. Makes 2–3 dozen cookies (depending on how thin you roll the dough).

much-deserved rest from the toils of everyday life. For them it was the time to relax and spend time with friends and family—and a chance to eat special dishes not prepared regularly throughout the year. The long-ago tradition of food and plenty has continued throughout the years . . . and may it continue for many, many more!

No Christmas would be complete without song.

SEVEN

Christmas Greetings
Song and Sentiment

CHRISTMAS GREETINGS

MERRY CHRISTMAS SERIES 403

A hundred years ago, Christmas postcards were common.

SINGING HAS always been part of human celebration, and some scholars believe that music may be one of the oldest Christmas customs. Many carols began as dance tunes. A chain of men and women holding hands moved to the music as the words were sung. From this merry singing and dancing have come some of our favorite Christmas carols, songs honoring Christ's birth and celebrating good will, peace, and hope among all people.

According to a legend from Oberndorf, Germany, the events that took place on the night of Christmas Eve 1818 gave us one of our most beloved Christmas carols. When the village church organ broke, the vicar of the church, Joseph Mohr wondered what to do for music for the Christmas Eve service. He wrote some lyrics during the day and his organist Franz Gruber composed the original melody for two voices and choir with guitar accompaniment. The song was complete in time for the midnight mass. "Silent Night" has since become the most recorded song of all time.

Swedish immigrants to North America brought with them the tradition of singing carols as family members join hands around their Christmas tree. Poland immigrants sang while the family walked around the tree. The *posada*, a tradition from Mexico, is a procession that goes from house to house asking permission to enter while singing a song. When they are refused, the guests say that they are Mary and Joseph, and then they are allowed in the house. (This tradition, like wassailing, which we discussed in chapter six, is a form of "mumming," a widespread European Christmas custom.)

Christmas carols are ageless. While most popular music endures only until it is replaced by newer songs, Christmas carols remain the same. The same carols sung by our ancestors are those we sing today. Like stories, we pass them down from generation to generation. Most people do not need a songbook; they have heard the lyrics again and again since they were children. Song is one way we express our joy at Christmas time.

The tradition of Christmas caroling is rooted in the ancient English custom of wassailing.

In 1910, Joyce Hall began selling picture postcards from two shoeboxes. By 1914 he replaced his postcards with greeting cards. After a large fire that destroyed their entire inventory, Hall and his brothers bought an engraving firm. The rest is history. Hallmark cards remained a mainstay in the greeting card industry and have included cards with the work of famous artists and writers including Norman Rockwell, Picasso, Grandma Moses, Marjolein Bastin, Maya Anjelou, and more.

The holiday season is a time when even the shyest and least demonstrative of us share how we feel about those we love. Today sentiments printed on cards are inscribed with messages of love, remembrance, and humor. Multicolor, elaborate designs are available in gift and card shops and even grocery stores. Cards can be sent electronically or personalized on your own computer.

The tradition of written greetings began a long time ago. In ancient Rome during Saturnalia festivals, clay tablets inscribed with good luck were exchanged. Sometimes even coins with special engravings wished others well. Although the first mass-produced Christmas card was commissioned by an English nobleman named Sir Henry Cole, individual Christmas greetings had been handwritten for years before.

In 1843, Sir Henry wanted to send greetings to friends but did not have the time to write each one individually. In desperation, he asked his friend, John Calcott Horsley to design a card that showed the feeding and clothing of the poor. Sir Henry sent 1,000 copies to his acquaintances that year.

In 1875, Louis Prang, a German immigrant, opened a **lithograph** shop in Roxbury, Massachusetts. His cards became an instant success, and by 1881 he produced 5 million Christmas cards. Most American cards featured Madonnas, angels, or children dressed for bed and awaiting the late-night visit of Santa Claus. By 1901, a revival of the old Roman plaques—

In 1836, Christmas became a legal holiday in the state of Alabama. But it wasn't until 1890 that all 50 states officially celebrated Christmas.

postcards—were sent, wishing recipients happy holidays. Postal rates had lowered by this time, and the mail service had become more dependable.

Exchanging cards at Christmas has become one of our cherished traditions. It allows us to keep in touch with people we may not hear from any other time of the year. Who hasn't waited to see the next year's picture of a growing family? Or read the yearly letter from an old friend? Remembering each other at Christmas is a gift of the heart.

Today Christmas continues to be a season of generous and loving traditions. Many give Charles Dickens the credit for teaching people the real meaning of Christmas. *A Christmas Carol*, first published in 1843, told the story of a greedy, miserly old man turned into a benevolent gift giver.

In North America, at the beginning of the 20th century, Santa Claus became the symbol for this spirit of Christmas generosity. In the early 1900s, people were focusing on children in a new way; the needs of children were given attention, and laws were passed that restricted or prohibited child labor. Out of this movement came the concept that every child had the right to a happy Christmas—and Santa Claus was the symbol of this universal

Charles Dickens read *A Christmas Carol* when he came to the United States in 1867. Tickets sold out quickly, and in Boston 10,000 tickets were sold weeks before his appearance. On stage he stood with only a podium, his book, and a glass of water. A couple who owned a business in Vermont closed their factory for the first time on Christmas Day after hearing Dickens's reading.

Santa Claus came to represent the 19th century's concern for children.

need. His image appeared everywhere—on greeting cards, in magazines, and in cartoons. Men dressed as Santa began to stand on street corners, ringing bells and collecting money for charities. Today, filling the Salvation Army kettles is still one of the more popular **philanthropies** during the Christmas season. Corner and mall kettles offer young and old the opportunity to give

American Legion members around Santa Claus, Indiana, read and answer more than 100,000 letters each year that children have written to Santa Claus.

Artist Thomas Nast helped create an image of a busy Santa taking requests for Christmas gifts.

A Christmas Carol, *Charles Dickens'* *tale of a haunted Christmas, changed the* *way North Americans looked at* *Christmas. Following Scrooge's example,* *many North Americans came to think of* *Christmas as a time for giving to* *strangers in need (as well as to loved* *ones).*

to those in need. Donations still reach children, both in North America and in poverty-stricken countries around the world. Contributions also benefit AIDS research and contribute to homeless shelters across North America.

Today, many people complain that Christmas has become commercialized to the point where it has lost its meaning. But Christmas continues to shine with a light that is deeper than marketing and Christmas sales. Across North American, Christmas is an occasion for love and joy, a time to reach out to others, a time to celebrate.

Further Reading

Chalmers, Irena. *The Great American Christmas Almanac*. New York: Viking, 1988.

Marling, Karal Ann. *Merry Christmas! Celebrating America's Greatest Holiday*. Cambridge, Mass.: Harvard University Press, 2000.

Nusom, Lynn. *Christmas in New Mexico: Recipes, Traditions, and Folklore for the Holiday Season*. Phoeniz, Ariz.: Golden West, 1991.

Pirotta, Saviour. *Joy to the World: Christmas Stories from Around the World*. New York: HarperCollins, 1998.

Sanna, Ellyn. *Favorite Christmas Traditions*. Uhrichsville, Ohio: Barbour, 1999.

Sanna, Ellyn. *Folk Holidays and Festivals*. Philadelphia: Mason Crest, 2003.

Shoemaker, Alfred. *Christmas in Pennsylvania*. Mechanicsburg, Penn.: Stackpole Books, 1999.

For More Information

Christmas Customs and Their Pagan Origens
www.serve.com/shea/germusa/pagan.htm

Christmas Fact and Folklore
www.delongfarms.com

Christmas History, Customs, and Legends
urbanlegends.about.com

How Christmas Works—The Complete Guide to Christmas Traditions
www.howstuffworks.com

Swedish Christmas Traditions
www.luth.se/luth/present/sweden/history/folklore/christmas.html

Glossary

Astrology   The study of the influence of stars on planets on human affairs.

Benevolence   Kindness and generosity.

Capon   A chicken.

Conservationist   Someone who works to guard the Earth's natural resources.

Cornucopias   Horn-shaped receptacles for fruit, grain, and other emblems of plenty.

Frankincense   A fragrant tree resin that was used for incense and embalming.

Lithograph   A form of printing that uses metal plates.

Magi   Wise people.

Martyred   Surrendered their life for a greater cause or belief.

Middle Ages   The period of European history from about AD 500 to 1500.

Mitered   Wearing the tall hat worn by bishops.

Mummers   Masked actors in English festivities.

Myrrh   A pungent-smelling tree resin.

Patron saint   A Catholic saint to whose protection and prayers a person or organization is dedicated.

Philanthropies   Charities.

Solstice   Either of the two days of the year (June 22 or December 22) when the sun is furthest from the celestial equator.

Index

Biographies

Sherry Bonnice lives in a log cabin on a dirt road in Montrose, Pennsylvania, with her husband, teenage daughter, five dogs, and 25 rabbits. She loves homeschooling her daughter, reading, and making quilts. Sherry has spent the last two years coediting three quilt magazines and writing a quilt book. Writing books for children and young people has been her dream.

Dr. Alan Jabbour is a folklorist who served as the founding director of the American Folklife Center at the Library of Congress from 1976 to 1999. Previously, he began the grant-giving program in folk arts at the National Endowment for the Arts (1974–76). A native of Jacksonville, Florida, he was trained at the University of Miami (B.A.) and Duke University (M.A., Ph.D.). A violinist from childhood on, he documented oldtime fiddling in the Upper South in the 1960s and 1970s. A specialist in instrumental folk music, he is known as a fiddler himself, an art he acquired directly from elderly fiddlers in North Carolina, Virginia, and West Virginia. He has taught folklore and folk music at UCLA and the University of Maryland and has published widely in the field.